Picture Credits:
Bridgeman Art Library: 18, 36 (Oldham Art Library), 37, 52 (top Science Museum), 54 (top Gavin Graham Gallery), 55; e.t. archive: 12-3, 44 (Science Museum), 50; Mary Evans Picture Library: 9, 13, 27, 43; Guildhall Library: 11; Hulton Picture Company: 5, 10, 15, 19, 20 (both), 22, 33, 48 (below), 52 (below); Image Bank: 30 below (P. Bartholomew/Liais), 58 (Jake Rajs), 59 (P&G Bowater); Mansell Collection: 40, 48 (top); Portfolio Pictures: cover, 6, 16, 39, 41 (National Portrait Gallery), 54 (below); Ann Ronan Picture Library: 4 (both), 7 (both), 19, 21, 23, 25, 28-9, 51 (below); Tate Gallery Publications: 30.

Published in Great Britain in 1992
by Exley Publications Ltd,
16 Chalk Hill, Watford,
Herts WD1 4BN, United Kingdom.

Copyright © Exley Publications, 1992
© Anna Sproule, 1991
**A copy of the CIP data is available from
the British Library**

ISBN 1-85015-254-3

Series editor: Helen Exley.
Picture research: Veneta Bullen.
Editing: Samantha Armstrong.
Typeset by Brush Off Studios,
St Albans, Herts AL3 4PH.
Printed and bound in Hungary.

James Watt

The story of the development of steam engines and how they created our industrial society

Anna Sproule

Nineteenth-century views of metal ore mining. The introduction of Watt's pumping engine in 1776 revolutionized the metal and coal mining industries, making it possible to extend the pits to areas that were previously too wet. The tall chimneys stand above the engine-houses that were built to operate the pumps.

Water, the enemy

The miners of Cornwall knew all about pumps. So did all the other men who earned their livings in the dark, hacking coal or metal ore out of the earth. Water – underground water – was one of their greatest enemies.

Ceaselessly, relentlessly, it oozed out of the earth below their feet, spouted out of the tunnel walls, and dripped down like rain from the tunnel roofs. Miners knelt in it, even lay in it to do their back-breaking work. And, if it was too deep, all work had to stop completely.

For centuries, this underground flood-water had been removed from mines by hand. The people who did it were children: children too small to wield a pick, yet still big enough to carry a bucket. But mines went on getting deeper – and wetter. And now, by the year 1777, machines had taken over.

Mines had gaunt machine pumps standing sentinel by the pit shafts. Powered by steam, their beams rocked and thumped from morning till night, pumping water up from the tunnels down below. The machine pumps were transforming the mining industry – but, even so, they had their drawbacks. They were cranky, unreliable, slow; they were dangerous if not carefully run. And, above all, they guzzled coal. The steam that worked them was produced by heating water until it boiled and, to do this, vast amounts of fuel were needed.

By 1776, the owners of Wheal Busy mine had decided that enough was enough. They'd heard of another type of pumping engine, an engine that worked faster and used less coal. It was the product of a business in Birmingham, called Boulton & Watt. The Wheal Busy owners ordered one and, next year, its component parts arrived. So did the man who would supervise the installation: James Watt himself, the new machine's inventor.

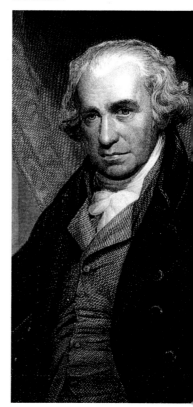

This engraving of James Watt is taken from a portrait painted when the carpenter's son had become a leading figure in science and industry. He had been elected a Fellow of the Royal Society, Britain's leading society of scientists.

The beam engine installed at Wheal Busy was one of the first of a long line of Watt engines. Watt's ambition was to adapt the action of the beam to produce rotary motion. By 1782 he had achieved this. The rotative beam engine shown here was built in 1788.

"The velocity, violence, magnitude and horrible noise of the engine give universal satisfaction to all beholders."

James Watt, describing reactions to his pumping engine.

Faster, cheaper, more powerful

In fact, Mr. Watt did not strike the Cornish miners as a very impressive figure. Nor had Cornwall been too impressed with his claims for his engine. But Wheal Busy would soon show Cornwall the truth, one way or the other. And now, in September 1777, the moment of truth had come.

In appearance, the Boulton & Watt machine looked very like the pump the Cornish knew already. But it worked faster, no doubt about that, and on much less fuel. How much less, the watchers gathered around the engine-house weren't yet sure. But it was something like a third of what they were used to; perhaps even a quarter. That meant the machine was going to make the mine-owners some big savings.

And no one who heard it in action could deny its power.

Deafened

The machine pounded on, emptying the flooded tunnel below and filling the Cornish miners with delight. Deafened as they were, the onlookers beamed. They clapped each other on the back, and shouted congratulations to their Scottish expert. Bowing and smiling, James Watt shouted something back. But the racket of his machine, thudding away behind him, snatched the words from his mouth and made them inaudible.

No matter, he thought wryly. The men around him would not – did not – understand anyway. They thought his achievement was all a matter of noise, size and cost-cutting. But the truth, he knew, was different.

Yes, certainly, he had cut their costs. Certainly, he had assaulted their ear-drums with the noise of the most powerful steam engine the world had ever known. But he also knew that he had changed the whole business of harnessing steam's enormous power to the service of its users.

What he did not know was that he had changed the world itself.

The baby that survived

James Watt was born on January 19, 1736 in Scotland, in the small port of Greenock near the mouth of the River Clyde. His father had originally trained as a carpenter and now built anything, from furniture to ships.

Mr. Watt's fine business sense and skills brought good money into the family's home. Although not rich, he and his wife Agnes were comfortably off. They needed that comfort, for their home life together was blighted by sadness. Agnes had baby after baby, and they all died.

When James was born, she re-doubled her efforts to protect her baby from the dozens of illnesses that threatened children then. This time, she succeeded and James – a thin, weakly little boy – survived. But his ailments survived with him. All through his childhood, he suffered from migraines and dreadful toothaches, and they condemned him

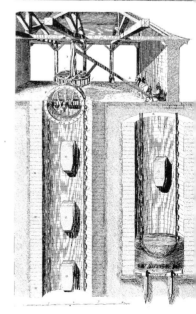

Prior to the steam age, energy for pumping and building operations had been provided by horse-power. In the top picture, a horse-gin is used to raise water from a well. As the horse moves in a circle, the gear-wheels operate a chain of water-containers. Below, horse-power is used to operate a pile-driver, sinking supports for a bridge into the soil below the river-bed.

to a sort of double life. One day, he'd be talkative, friendly, interested in everyone and everything around him; the next, he'd be lost in a haze of pain.

Playground bullies

He was obviously bright but, at first, his migraines stopped him attending school. So his parents – themselves highly intelligent – started educating him at home. Agnes taught him to read; her husband, busy though he was, made time to give him lessons in writing and arithmetic. He also gave him a small carpentry set; armed with miniature saws and chisels, the boy took all his toys to pieces, put them together again, and then invented new ones.

James spent a childhood as happy as his troubled health would allow. But, when he was eleven, his happiness came to an end when he finally went to school. The move was a disaster. Nothing in his sheltered life had prepared him for this: for the noise, for the teasing and fights, for the endless rough-and-tumble of the schoolyard.

He didn't understand the jokes; he couldn't join in the games. For protection, he shrank into himself, but found no refuge there. Instead, he became a natural target for the playground bullies. He escaped them when, aged thirteen, the nightmare came to an end and he changed schools. But the marks those two years set on him – shyness, self-distrust, a certainty that things would turn out badly – would only leave him when, respected and wealthy, he reached old age.

His gifts surface again

All the same, the worst of James' miseries was now behind him. In the safer, calmer surroundings of Greenock Grammar School, he plucked up courage to let his gifts surface again. Quickly, he blossomed into an outstanding mathematician. Out of school, he started learning the family trade.

He had fully inherited his father's skill with his hands; it seemed he could make anything, out of almost any material. But the thing he did best was

"James, I never saw such an idle boy! Take a book or employ yourself usefully. For the last half hour you have not spoken a word, but taken off the lid of that kettle and put it on again, holding now a cup and now a silver spoon over the steam; watching how it rises from the spout, and catching and counting the drops of water."
James Watt's aunt, talking to her nephew in 1750.

"Every evening before ten o'clock, our usual hour of retiring to rest, he contrives to engage me in conversation, then begins some striking tale, and, whether humorous or pathetic, the interest is so overpowering, that the family all listen to him with breathless attention, and hour after hour strikes unheeded."
Teenage James Watt on a visit; described to his mother by his hostess.

precise, delicate metalwork.

Much of Mr. Watt's business dealt with Greenock's main industry, shipping. He was a ship-owner and merchant as well as a builder, and his stock-in-trade included navigation aids like quad-rants, compasses and telescopes. James learned how to use them, then how to repair them. And, by his mid-teens, his mind was made up. He wanted to be a maker of scientific instruments, not a carpenter nor a shipwright.

It was easier said than done. Making scientific instruments was highly skilled work, and demanded a long training. But who was there in Greenock to train him? The answer was nobody. But Glasgow, where his mother had come from, looked more promising. So, in 1754, James left home to see what the university city had to offer.

In one way he had luck. Agnes Watt's maiden name had been Muirhead and, in Glasgow, the Muirheads were good people to know. One of them,

As a boy, James Watt's shyness and poor health led him to develop his intellectual gifts, and one of these was a spirit of inquiry. This famous painting by Marcus Stone shows the young Watt observing the condensation of steam as it emerged from a boiling kettle, an incident which one of his aunts remembered happening. The story led to the myth, quite untrue, that Watt had the idea of the steam-engine while sitting at home at the tea-table.

George Muirhead, taught at the university. It was thanks to this university connection that Watt made the contacts, which – then and later – would shape his life.

One of them, a scientist, Robert Dick, was especially impressed by the young man, and even gave him a temporary job, arranging and setting up an array of scientific instruments. So far, so good; but, when it came to getting proper training, Watt found he was no further forward than he'd been in Greenock. There was no one in the city who could do it.

London-bound

Dick, however, came to his rescue. Watt, he said, was wasting his time; London was the place to be. Back in Greenock, Watt's father – who had fallen on hard times – agreed to the plan. Robert Dick wrote to a London instrument maker that he knew, urging him to take Watt on as a trainee. And Watt himself packed his possessions, put them on a London-bound ship, bought a horse and set out on the long road south. It took him twelve days.

He arrived in mid-June 1755, and hurried straight to meet Dr. Dick's contact. But, to his dismay, he had no luck. Dick's friend, James Short, was everything Dick had said: decent, helpful, friendly, and a leading practitioner of his craft. But he could not take Watt into his business. Nor could anyone else.

The young man trudged around the city for two weeks, visiting one likely source of training after another. Every time, it was the same story. James Watt had come up against a formidable obstacle: the Worshipful Company of Clock-makers.

Trapped in a vicious circle

The Worshipful Company was the body that laid down all the rules governing London's instrument-making trade. Qualified instrument-makers, one of these rules said, could only take two sorts of people into their business: other qualified instrument-makers, or apprentices serving the seven-year

Clock, watch and instrument makers guarded their craft jealously and kept down the number of trainees so that their skills would be more highly valued. In the eighteenth century, every part of every instrument had to be made using hand-tools and the work demanded great accuracy and concentration.

training period that the trade demanded.

Watt was *not* qualified; nor, unless a London business took him on, did he stand a chance of becoming so. But the only way to qualifications led through an apprenticeship. And Watt, by now almost twenty, was too old to start one.

He was trapped in a vicious circle of regulations. He'd come all this way for nothing – and there was nothing for him back home, either. Meanwhile, his money was running out.

Just when things were looking their worst, Dick's friend Short came up with another contact to try. His name was John Morgan, his trade was brasswork, and he had a business off Cornhill, in the very heart of the City of London. Unlike the others, Morgan took a devil-may-care attitude to the Worshipful Company's rules. Young Watt, he said, was welcome to join his business – at a price. The trainee was to work for his master free of charge for a year; on top of that, he was to pay Morgan a "training fee".

Free of charge ... a training fee ... It did not

"We work to nine o'clock every night, except Saturdays."
James Watt, writing to his father from London, 1756.

Cornhill, in the City, as it was when Watt eventually found work in this area of London. John Morgan gave Watt the chance to break into an apprenticeship but worked him so hard that Watt saw little of his environment.

Above: Before steam power created the Industrial Revolution, farming was the main activity in all national economies. Whole farming communities revolved round the local markets and fairs.

Opposite: The press-gangs were ruthless. If they saw a man fit enough to join up they would accept no excuses. This Thames waterman was kidnapped on Tower Hill in London on the morning of his wedding day.

sound ideal, but Watt jumped at the chance.

Morgan – no fool – had instantly spotted how talented Watt was. By August, the unofficial trainee had caught up with and passed Morgan's official apprentice, who had been there two years. By the following spring, when Watt graduated to surveying instruments, like theodolites, even he could admit to himself that he was good.

Over-worked, under-nourished

But James Watt was paying a high price for his success. His headaches, which had eased in his early teens, had now come back – and no wonder. Frantic to cram several years' training into one, the young man worked a ten-hour day for Morgan. Then, exhausted as he was, he'd get up very early to fit

in some extra work: work that brought in a tiny amount of cash. Together with what his father could afford to send him, this brought him an income of eight shillings a week. Even at near-starvation level, it was barely enough to live on.

Over-worked and under-nourished, he was also desperately short of exercise and fresh air. Both would have done him good, but he didn't dare take them. At that time, Britain was at war with France. The British Navy constantly wanted men – and they didn't wait for people to volunteer! To make up shortages, press-gangs scoured the streets and kidnapped any likely-looking man they could find. Often, he was never seen again.

Watt, thin and ailing as he was, would have been fair game. So, month after month, he stayed indoors, in Morgan's cold workshops.

So much for London's promises

Watt completed his training year in triumph. And then, in the summer of 1756, his health broke down completely. Rheumatism, migraines, crushing fatigue: all set on him and would not let go.

So much for London and all its promises; he had to get home. With his clothes, tools and a precious book on instrument-making packed in his saddlebags, twenty-year-old James Watt slowly made his way back up the Great North Road, to Scotland and to Greenock.

Once back, Watt recovered quickly. He recovered his spirits as well and, later that year, returned to Glasgow. Here he found that Robert Dick had a splendid project waiting for him. A valuable collection of astronomical instruments had recently arrived from Jamaica – but the weeks at sea in a salt-laden atmosphere had done the delicate metalwork no good. Watt was given the job of setting the instruments to rights.

He was paid five pounds for it – a handsome sum at that time. But his real reward lay in the work itself, and in the new friends he made while he was doing it.

The Jamaica collection fascinated Glasgow's scientists, who often came to watch the work. Naturally, they also got to know the technician in charge and, to their surprise, they found he was as knowledgeable as any university man.

Coming out of his shell

One of Watt's new acquaintances was a student of mathematics and mechanics, John Robison. Another – at the other end of the university's social scale – was Joseph Black, a hugely-distinguished scientist who'd just been appointed professor of chemistry.

In spite of his grand reputation, Black was himself a young man: in fact, only ten years older than Robison. The professor and the pupil, who first met in Watt's workshop, got on brilliantly – and they got on just as well with Watt, who came between them in age. Black liked the gifted technician's

---

"He [James Watt] was as remarkable for the goodness of his heart, and the candour and simplicity of his mind, as for the acuteness of his genius and understanding."

Professor Black.

"I had the vanity to think myself a pretty good proficient in my favourite study, and was rather mortified at finding Mr. Watt so much my superior. But his own high relish for those things made him pleased with the chat of any person who had the same tastes with himself.... I lounged much about him, and, I doubt not, was frequently teasing him. Thus our acquaintance began."

John Robison, describing how he first met James Watt.

"simplicity" and good nature. Robison – a cheerful, bantering character – became Watt's friend on the spot. The banter, the admiration and, above all, the shared delight in science brought Watt right out of his shell, and laid the foundations of friendships that would last a lifetime.

The following year, Watt decided to set up as an instrument-maker in the city he now saw as his home. It must have been a sickening shock to find that, in one way at least, Glasgow was just like London. The Glasgow craftsmen also had their city tightly sewn up.

Watt was not a Glasgow man, nor had he served his apprenticeship in Glasgow. The message he received from the other Glasgow instrument-makers was clear: intruders, keep out!

Promptly, his university friends came to his help, just as they had done before he went to London. And, this time, they changed the course of his life.

The Glasgow craftsmen had no power over what happened in the university precincts, nor over people employed by the university itself. The astute professors arranged things so that Watt could set up shop in the university grounds. And they made it official by giving him the title of "Mathematical Instrument Maker to the University".

Part of things

James Watt of Greenock, who'd come up by the most uncertain and unofficial of routes, was an outsider no longer. From then on, he was part of things: part of the great stream of scientific interest and achievement that was flooding through Britain and the western world. The only trouble was – it did not bring him enough to live on.

Resourcefully, Watt studied his market, and decided to enlarge the scope of his business. He would make musical instruments as well as scientific ones. He didn't have the slightest ear for music; if anything, he disliked it. But he was totally at home in music's first cousin, mathematics. Soon, an amazing range of instruments began coming out of his workshops: harps, flutes, bagpipes, and even

Dr. Joseph Black arrived as professor of chemistry at Glasgow University only shortly before James Watt joined the university as an instrument maker. The two quickly became close friends.

15

organs. And not merely the standard type of organ, either, but an improved model.

As a child, Watt had taken his toys to pieces and re-fashioned them to make new ones. Now, as an adult, the urge to tinker, to improve, to explore was as strong as ever. So the stops on a Watt organ functioned more efficiently than they did on the traditional type; a Watt organ made better, more economic use of the air pumped through it.

A tricky job

Two years later, when Watt was still in his early twenties, a prosperous and friendly architect gave him the backing to open another shop, in the city itself. This time, the other Glasgow instrument-makers didn't raise a murmur and, by 1763, Watt's business had grown big enough for him to take on apprentices of his own. But he still kept up his links with the university, where his first shop stayed open. And it was to this shop that Professor John Anderson came in the winter of 1763 with a repair job that needed doing.

By this time, Watt's first patron, Dr. Dick, had died. Anderson was his successor, and he was just as impressed by Watt as Dick had been. He explained to the technician that the job he wanted done now was an especially tricky one. In fact, it had already defeated an instrument-maker in London.

Watt, always hungry for problems to solve, accepted the challenge eagerly. And Anderson handed this latest problem over – a model of a Newcomen pump.

A Newcomen pump! Watt knew of it, naturally. So did anyone who, in the eighteenth century, took an interest in machines and what they could do. What the pump had done went far beyond its day-to-day job of emptying flooded mines. Without it, in fact, the mining industry would never have been transformed from a pick-and-scratch activity to the booming industry it had become.

But Watt had another reason for his interest. He was interested in the unusual way the pump was powered. Unusual? It was revolutionary.

Opposite: The original building of Glasgow University, in the heart of the city, was known as the "Old College". It was in this building that James Watt, as a technician in the Natural Philosophy department, made the all-important contacts that launched him on his career as an engineer. In the nineteenth century the University was moved to a new site and the Old College was demolished.

Throughout history, farmers, craftspeople, and soldiers had been inventing and improving tools to help them do their jobs. But, until less than a hundred years before, they had known only three main methods of powering those tools: of transmitting energy to them so that they performed the work they were designed for.

Muscles, wind and water

The oldest and simplest cheapest method was muscle power itself – the movements of a farmer cutting corn, or a blacksmith hammering a horseshoe. The horse that wore it provided another source of muscle power, as did donkeys and oxen. Animals like these were stronger than humans, and animal power was used in all sorts of ways – such as working the fields, grinding corn, pulling carts, or drawing water from wells.

However, horses were expensive animals, and only the wealthy used them often. And all animal power was expensive in one way, for the animals themselves needed constant attention. They needed housing, doctoring, and feeding – especially feeding. Two other sources of power were much simpler and less time-consuming to service, once the equipment had been set up. They were wind and water.

Wind, captured in the sails of a windmill, was as good as a horse for turning millstones or pumping up water from underground. Water, channelled over slatted water-wheels placed across a stream, could turn millstones and other equipment in just the same way. And wind and water, brought together in the sailing ship, provided one of the most efficient transport methods then known. James Watt might have opted for the land route to London, but plenty of other people preferred a sea journey to the horrors of travel on Europe's appalling roads.

Natural power

Muscle power, wind power, water power: each one, properly harnessed and used, could be highly efficient in its way. They still are. In hot countries with thin, fragile soils, a traditional bullock-harrow damages the land much less than a western-style tractor. Meanwhile, in countries with fast-flowing rivers, hydro-electric plants generate electricity for millions of homes.

Human muscle power cut and carted coal from the beginning of the industry into the nineteenth century. Because of the narrowness of the tunnels, children were often given the task of hauling laden tubs of coal.

Opposite: Thomas Savery's "Miner's Friend" was the first steam pump, and it was quickly put to use in coal pits.

But all three sources of power have one thing wrong with them. They are ultimately controlled, not by their users, but by nature. The wind can drop; the river that works a water-wheel can dry up in summer, freeze in winter. If a living being is worked too hard, it collapses from exhaustion. And what happens in places where there are no handy streams, no sources of fodder for grazing oxen?

For most of history, the users of powered equipment accepted these problems as facts of life. There was nothing they could do about them, except make

.the best of whatever fate sent. And then, at the very end of the 1600s, something happened that would one day abolish this servitude for good. In Britain, Thomas Savery announced that he had solved the problem of the flooded mines.

The world's first pump

Savery's solution was a pump – but a pump like none other. It worked independently of wind, weather and the aching muscles of tired children or animals. It would go on working as hard and as long as its operators wished. He called it an "engine to raise water by fire".

It was not, in fact, powered by fire, but by water heated to boiling point over a fire: water that had been turned into steam. Savery's "Miner's Friend", which he patented in 1698, was the world's first practical steam engine.

Breakthrough though it was, the pump was not the first steam-powered machine the world had ever seen. As far back as the first century AD, a Greek, Hero of Alexandria, had described the workings of a toy steam turbine: a machine that twirled round and round as steam inside it escaped.

What made Hero's toy work was the way water behaves when it is boiled and vaporized: it expands about seventeen hundred times. But later, investigators found there was another method of using steam to drive machinery, and they experimented with that as well.

This other method relied, not just on the effects of heating water, but also on what happened when the vaporized water was suddenly cooled again. The result was a sudden vacuum: a vacuum that would be instantly filled by any liquid or gas that had access to it.

Using this second method, Savery had designed a machine to suck a liquid – water – up from a flooded mine. It was a beautifully-simple idea, and it ought to have worked. Unfortunately, the design was a little too simple. The machine only worked at shallow depths – and, if it was worked too hard – it blew up!

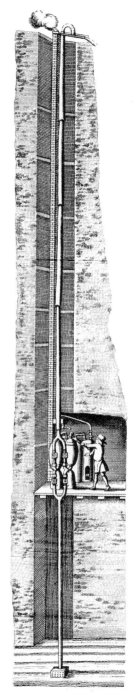

It was not long, however, before a second pump came on the scene that worked very well indeed. Its inventor was a blacksmith, and his name was Thomas Newcomen.

The Newcomen pump

The "atmospheric engine" that Newcomen set up in 1712 was far more complex than Savery's machine. With its great domed boiler, brick engine house and gaunt, see-sawing beam connected with the heavy pump rods, it was also very much bigger. Its heart was a tall iron cylinder, open at the top and standing over the boiler. When the water boiled, the cylinder filled with the steam it made.

Although the cylinder was open at the top, it had a kind of moving "lid" inside. This was a piston: a circular plate that, although packed with leather to fit the cylinder exactly, was still free to slide up and down. It was attached to a vertical rod – the piston rod – and this, in turn, was fastened to one end of the pump's "handle": the rocking-beam balanced overhead.

When the cylinder below the piston was filled with steam, the weight of the pump rods pulled the other end of the beam down. At the cylinder end, the beam rose up and, at the same time, the piston was dragged up to rest just inside the cylinder's rim.

Pulling the "pump-handle" down meant pushing the piston down to the bottom of the cylinder again. This was where the vacuum method came in, but Newcomen used this method with a difference.

When the steam condensed

The vacuum produced by the cooling, condensing steam in his pump did not act directly to move anything up or down. Instead, the opposite took place. The vacuum made it possible for the moving to be done by something else: by the air.

To cool the steam in his machine, Newcomen sprayed the inside of the cylinder with cold water. The steam condensed, making a vacuum. There was now literally nothing in the cylinder, so the atmosphere outside it – the air – could exert its own pressure on the piston, driving it far down into the cylinder's interior. And, as the piston moved down, it dragged the rocking-beam down with it.

The pump-handle moved into the "down" position. Then, when steam entered the cylinder again to destroy the vacuum, it moved up again. And down. And up – and down again, as long as the machinery and the fuel supply could hold out.

Savery had pointed the way. But it was

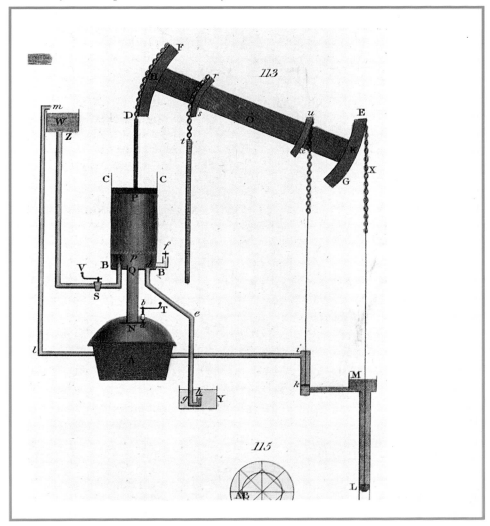

blacksmith Thomas Newcomen who had actually given the world its first real alternative to the sources of power it had known for so long. In doing so, he had started a process that would, one day, transform that world for ever.

When the machine stopped

James Watt, technical adviser to the University of Glasgow, certainly knew all about the Newcomen pump. But he'd never actually seen one. Delighted, he took the model from Anderson, set it up on his workbench and examined it: its beam and pump rod, its tiny boiler, its neatly-tooled cylinder with its piston and valves.

He soon located the problems that had baffled the London man, and set to work. As winter settled in, the job neared completion and, at last, the little pump stood repaired and ready for testing.

Robison was there to watch the tests take place. The boiler was filled, the fire below it was lit, and the steam began to build up. Then, with the two men watching intently, the little piston began to plunge up and down, pivoting the beam fixed to the strut above.

It worked; it was working well. Four strokes … five strokes … six…. Watt and Robison smiled with satisfaction as the machine puttered on.

And then the puttering stopped.

Not enough steam …

What was this? The model had been working well enough, so what had gone wrong? Watt tried one thing after the other – stoking up the fire, raising the level of the minute water-tank, perched high above the apparatus. But nothing made any difference. The model, as repaired, certainly worked; but it only worked for a few strokes.

As Watt's experiments on the model went on, he began to realize what had happened. It was not his workmanship that was at fault. The fault lay in the pump's design. The full-scale Newcomen engine was notorious for the greedy way it consumed fuel.

The strange way the model behaved was caused by a similar greed. Its miniature boiler could not produce enough steam to work the pump.

The model was now as close to working order as it ever could be. But, to a problem-lover like Watt, the puzzles it had set couldn't be given up so easily. Why, for instance, did the machine need so much fuel, use so much steam? How much steam *did* it use, anyway?

There was only one way to find out: by trying things out for himself. So, step by experimental step, Watt began to piece together the laws that governed steam and the way it behaved. And, as he did so, he realized just what was wrong with Newcomen's original design.

... and too much heat

Both the miniature model and the fuel-greedy engine itself used far, far too much heat. They could not help it. With every stroke of the engine, the steam-filled cylinder had to be cooled to the point

It was his study of a model of the Newcomen engine in his Glasgow laboratory that led James Watt to design an improved version which was more reliable and used less fuel.

where the steam condensed. Then, right away, the cylinder had to be heated up again: heated up by the steam rushing into it from below, heated to the point where that steam did not condense, but remained steam.

No wonder the model pump had not worked. It simply could not cope with all the heating and re-heating! And no wonder the full-sized atmospheric engine used such vast quantities of fuel.

In spite of its great value and even greater promise, the world's first effective steam-engine was flawed. It was flawed by waste, by inefficiency, by a gross error in its design. James Watt, with his gift for creative improvements, had at last found a challenge worthy of his talents.

Everything turned on the way the vacuum was created. It was produced by condensing the steam that had rushed into the cylinder. To produce it, that steam had to be suddenly cooled – by the water sprayed from the machine's injection jet. And the cylinder, of course, cooled too.

Was there any way of producing a vacuum *without* cooling the cylinder? That was the problem. Watt turned it over in his mind for months, sketching in one solution after another. But none of them worked. Every time, he was brought up short by the central conundrum: no cooling, no vacuum. No vacuum, no pump – and no steam power.

A walk on Glasgow Green

The real solution, when it came to him, came suddenly: between one breath and the next. Between one step and the next, for he was taking a Sunday afternoon walk.

It was a beautiful, sweet-scented afternoon in May – May 1765. A gentle wind blew, shaking the bushes around Glasgow Green. The green was really a big meadow on the riverbank, close-grazed by sheep. The washerwomen of Glasgow came here to bleach their sheets in the sun; outside working hours, everyone else came here too, to walk by the river and enjoy the fresh air. Spruce in his Sunday best, and driven from his workbench by the strict

Scottish rules against working on Sunday, James Watt had come to take the air like the others.

He was now a married man but, this afternoon, his wife Margaret had stayed at home. Wandering along on his own, deep in thought, he passed the building the washerwomen used, then the house where the shepherd lived.

And then, all at once, he thought of it: the answer to the riddle, the solution to the whole problem.

The separate container

Steam had no shape. It was fluid, elastic. Because of this, it would rush into any empty container: into any container that enclosed a vacuum. Now, supposing a container like this were attached to the engine's cylinder? A container equipped with an injection jet?

The steam would rush into that, *and be cooled there.* That was where the all-important cooling and condensing process would take place – in a separate

By the eighteenth century, Glasgow had become Scotland's second city. Its prosperity was based on the goods that passed through its port, which was conveniently placed for the growing shipping trade across the Atlantic. This provided work not only for dock workers, but also for merchants, and for an army of clerks to keep track of imports and exports.

part of the engine altogether.

As the steam condensed, more steam would come rushing in, to be condensed in its turn. And yet more steam would rush in, and more, until all the steam in the cylinder had been sucked into the condensing chamber. And all that would then be left in the still-hot cylinder would be … a vacuum.

He had found it! The separate container, the condenser: that was the key to the puzzle that had been taunting him for so long. That was how he could produce the vacuum needed for the pumping action, and keep the cylinder hot at the same time. Now, how could he get rid of the water once it was condensed…?

Chafing with impatience, Watt went home and, somehow, got through the rest of the Sabbath. First thing on Monday morning, he was at his workbench, working frantically with a soldering iron. Gone was the time for meticulous, painstaking craft skills. Today, improvization ruled.

He needed something – something small and round – to stop one end of a pipe. He raided his wife's sewing basket, and used her thimble.

He needed a strong, well-crafted brass cylinder. Rather than waste time making one, he used the cylinder from a big brass syringe. Its normal use was injecting wax into dead bodies, to prepare them for dissection by the university's medical students. But no matter; it would do just as well here.

Under Watt's hands, a tiny pump began to take place: a pump like none other, a strange, upside-down object, with the piston near the foot of the cylinder and the protruding piston rod ending in a hook.

The principle of the vacuum – essential to the steam engine – was proved by this experiment. The hemispheres (opposite) were clamped together and the air pumped out of them. Two teams of horses could not pull them apart.

29

Within a few years, the Industrial Revolution changed the entire face of the countryside. Areas close to coalfields were heavily built-up with factories and housing for factory workers who were attracted by higher wages than they could earn in farming. Farming areas lost much of their population to the towns – a process that continues today.

It moves!

At last, he had finished. The connections were all made, and a test weight dangled on the end of the piston rod. Through a pipe connected with a temporary boiler, steam was hissing into the cylinder: a tightly-closed one, with a double skin that was itself being filled with steam.

When wisps of steam appeared from the top, he knew everything was ready. Carefully, he turned off the connection; carefully, too, he pumped air out of the condenser and cooled it with water. Inside, a vacuum would have formed, sucking steam out of the upper part of the cylinder and creating a vacuum there too...

And then, before his delighted gaze, it happened. The test weight on the end of the rod began to move. It moved upward, pulled closer and closer to the cylinder by the piston rod. Meanwhile, the rod itself was vanishing into the cylinder's interior. It was being pushed in by the steam that had collected *below* the piston: steam that, like air, exerted a pressure against the piston's surface and drove it upward into the vacuum that had been created above. And, all the time, the cylinder itself was kept hot: boiling hot, steaming hot, heated by the "steam jacket" that formed its double skin.

He had done it.

"A perfect steam-engine"

John Robison was away from Glasgow during the weekend of his friend's great invention. He came back later, full of fresh ideas about the riddle that he'd left Watt chewing on. Hurrying around to Watt's home, he found him in a strange mood.

When Robison arrived, Watt was sitting by the fire with a small tin box on his knees. Beside him, a soldering iron was heating on the flames. Robison chattered on but Watt – usually so warm, so enthusiastic – made little response. Staring into the fire, he seemed far away.

At last, putting the box on the floor, he cut Robison's chatter short. "You need not fash yourself any more about that, man," he said, in his broad

"The fortunate thought occurred to him [Watt] of condensing the steam by cold in a separate vessel or apparatus, between which and the cylinder a communication was to be opened for that purpose every time the steam was to be condensed; while the cylinder itself might be preserved perpetually hot.... This capital improvement flashed on his mind at once, and filled him with rapture."

Professor Black, recalling the invention of the separate condenser.

John Roebuck takes a hand

Without delay, the professor introduced Watt and his invention to John Roebuck: scientist, industrialist, and lease-holder on the rich coal deposits that lay at Kinneil near Edinburgh. Watt – so Black thought – could put his pump at Roebuck's disposal. In return, Roebuck would give him the backing, premises, and encouragement he needed to bring it from its trial stage to full working use.

It was a good plan, but it never quite came off. True, Watt succeeded in building a full-scale version of his pumping engine, and setting it up at Kinneil. But, over the next nine years, that was about as far as things went.

Part of the fault was Watt's. He hated having to act the boss and run a team of workers. He didn't like the business of keeping on good terms with his new patron: at the wrong moments, he would turn shy and prickly.

Roebuck, however, was at fault, too. He knew all about Watt's need for a steady income. But, for some time, he did nothing himself to help ease his partner's financial problems. Instead, he actually encouraged Watt in a plan to leave instrument-making and set up as a surveyor.

Gathering dust

Perhaps he hoped to get Watt "on the cheap", by making sure that – when not working on the pump – he was doing a job that paid well. But, if so, Roebuck was out in his reckoning. Watt's career change took him all over the country and, in his workroom at Kinneil, his invention gathered cobwebs and dust.

All the same, Roebuck did Watt two services that were genuinely valuable. First, he helped Watt take out a patent on his machine. This meant that, for the years of the patent's life, no one could copy the method Watt had invented for "lessening the consumption of steam and fuel in fire engines."

The patent itself, which was granted in 1769, formed part of the financial deal that Roebuck and Watt eventually made: Roebuck was to pay off

Watt's old debt to Black and, in return, would take two-thirds of any money the invention made.

Roebuck's second service was even more important. At long distance, he introduced Watt to the man who, more than anyone else, ensured that Watt's invention reached the public: Matthew Boulton of Birmingham.

Matthew Boulton's "Manufactory"

Boulton, like Roebuck, was a wealthy industrialist. The business he had inherited from his father made ornamental metal goods. By the 1760s, the fashionable world had taken up pierced steelwork as its latest fad, and Boulton supplied everything the fashionable world could need; ornamental buttons, watch-chains, combs, sword hilts, and snuff boxes.

Production on this wide scale was then very unusual, for most craft work – like that of Watt himself – was still slow, small-scale and workshop-based. But Boulton would have none of that. He had decided to house all his craft workers under one roof, in a "Manufactory": in a manufactory, moreover, that was fitted out with all the latest, most efficient equipment money could buy.

This was revolutionary enough, for the idea of a large-scale, centralized workplace was then extremely new – almost unheard-of. But Boulton had then gone one better by building the biggest factory in the western world.

The chance of a lifetime

Watt and Boulton met for the first time in August 1768 and, from the start, they got on splendidly. Boulton – jovial, confident, successful and shrewd – took an instant liking to the engineer and surveyor who was none of those things. Watt, for his part, relaxed in the warmth of Boulton's friendliness, and responded with delight to his interest in the steam-engine. For Boulton, the man who'd had the vision to spend a fortune on his new-style premises, was very interested indeed.

With a sharp eye for good business deals, he

Canal-building was the main work of civil engineers in the eighteenth century. Surveying and planning a canal demanded a high degree of accuracy to ensure a good and continuous water supply. The positioning of locks, enabling canal vessels to change levels, was critical. During Watt's six years as a canal surveyor, he invented a micrometer for judging distances and heights.

realized he was facing the chance of a lifetime. Watt's pump – if it worked – was obviously the answer to the mine-owners prayers. Nor were they the only ones who desperately needed an efficient pump; nor, come to that, was pumping the only work Watt's engine could do!

Manufacturing the Scotsman's machine would be a highly profitable business; Boulton was sure of it. So would Watt like to do business with him?

Poor Watt! Earlier, he'd have jumped at the chance – but now he was tied to Roebuck by his debts and agreements. For a while, the three men tried to negotiate a deal that pleased everyone, but the negotiations fell through. Dispirited and poorly, Watt went on working for a while on the Kinneil project. And then, in 1771, he abandoned it completely. He spent the next few years as a full-time surveyor, constructing canals all over Scotland.

The final blow?

Fruitlessly, Roebuck begged him to come back; the inquiries that reached Watt from Birmingham made no difference either. He could fight against circumstances no longer. He had to provide for himself, his wife, and their three children; he had to earn a practical, day-to-day living. The love-affair with the steam-engine was over. He was through.

And then, in March, 1773, Roebuck went bankrupt.

To thirty-seven-year-old Watt, it must have seemed like the final blow: the end to his lifetime's great dream. But it was, in fact, the very opposite. The way now lay open for Boulton to take on Roebuck's two-thirds share in the patent – which, in August, he did.

The next month, something happened that finally shook Watt free from surveying, Scotland, and his roots for ever.

In September 1774, his wife, Margaret, was pregnant again. As gales swept the Highlands, word reached her surveyor husband that she was desperately ill. Watt set out at once on a nightmarish journey back to Glasgow, riding post-haste through the storm. But, fast as he could travel, he arrived too late. Margaret was dead, and her baby with her.

It was Margaret who had played as great a part as his friends in keeping his spirits up during the difficult years, urging him to keep faith with himself. "I beg you would not make yourself uneasy, though things should not succeed to your wish," she had once written to him. "If it [the steam engine] will not do, something else will. Never despair."

Next spring, when his grief eased, Watt packed up his belongings and headed south: to Birmingham, where people wanted him, and where his future lay.

Going public

It was March again: a Friday in early March 1776. And the owners and directors of the Bentley Mining Company were nerving themselves to view their newest piece of equipment.

Before the "railway explosion" of the nineteenth century, canal and river transport was vitally important to many communities the world over. In remote areas, where it would have been expensive to build roads for a small amount of traffic, inland water was the main means of transporting passengers as well as goods.

Would it work? Would it work as well as they hoped? Would it prove them right in their decision to scrap their half-built Newcomen pump and go for this latest model? Or would their new pumping engine make fools of them all: of Mr. Bentley and his colleagues, of the inventor and his partner, and of all the distinguished crowd of visitors who, even now, were thronging in to see the machine work?

They'd have been more nervous still if they'd known the press was present too. A correspondent of the local paper was already composing lines in his head as, eyes bright and ears open, he moved among the assembled crowd. The Boulton & Watt pumping engine – capable, so it was said, of emptying a mine three hundred feet deep – was about to make its first-ever public performance, and no one wanted to miss the show.

"Many years Study"

From every side, details rained down on the correspondent. Watt pumping engines, he was told, were very different from anything that had been seen before. They used only a quarter – a quarter! it was almost unbelievable – of the fuel a Newcomen engine would need to do a similar job. They had taken their inventor years of work to develop "many years Study," as the newspaper later said, "and a great Variety of expensive and laborious Experiments."

The cylinder, the correspondent learned, was fifty inches across, and had been made by the best ironmaster in all Britain, John Wilkinson. Not long ago, Wilkinson had invented a way of making cannon barrels so that they were perfectly round inside – all along their length. He'd now brought the same skill to bear on making the central component of the Boulton & Watt engine. Indeed, he'd gone one better, and installed a Watt machine at his own premises to act as a gigantic bellows.

Of course, all the precision work – the valves, pistons, connections and the condenser itself – had come, not from Wilkinson's but from Birmingham: from the great Soho Manufactory itself, where Watt and Boulton now reigned in partnership. The

Bloomsfield machine was the second to emerge from the special section that Boulton had set up at Soho to house the new enterprise. Four more steam-engines, the newspaper correspondent learned, were nearly ready, and more were planned.

The beam swings down

Around Bloomfield's new engine-house, the excited crowd thickened, swirled, finally stood still. Inside, sweating in the machine's heat, an engineer danced nimbly around before the towering equipment, pulling levers, opening and closing valves. Above him, like the jutting arm of a gallows, loomed the great beam that, see-sawing on its pivot, would act as the handle to work the new pump.

News of the success of the Bentley Colliery engine spread fast, and soon orders were pouring in to Boulton's Soho factory. This pumping engine was installed in 1777 for the Birminghan Canal Navigations, a year after the Bentley prototype started work.

Boulton's Soho Manufactory in Birmingham, England, where he and Watt set up a special department to make parts for their engines. Working methods at Soho were very advanced for their time. The usual plan in industry was for workers to make a range of different items. Boulton saw that if they specialized on one particular item they would develop their skills and work more efficiently.

Deftly, the engineer closed a sequence of valves in turn, checked a gauge, pulled a lever, then paused. Finally, he stretched out his arm and opened a new valve.

And, high overhead, the giant pump-handle suddenly swung downward.

Down it came – "the length of the Stroke is 7 feet" noted the newspaper correspondent – and up it went again. And down it plunged, and up, and down, all with great thudding strokes. The chains clanked, the wooden timbers creaked and groaned, the walls of the engine-house shook with the din. Deafened and entranced, the crowd watched the beam's hypnotic rise and fall.

Meanwhile, down in the water-logged pit, the level of the water began to drop.

Dawn of the Age of Steam

In less than an hour, the show was over. The pit, which had once stood fifty-seven feet deep in water, was now empty. The great beam made its last descent; the engineer closed off valves and shut the machine down. The crowd, chattering excitedly, made its way off to the celebration dinner that had been provided.

. Behind them, the Bentley Company's new purchase stood silent again, awaiting the moment when it would be put to work in earnest. But its greatest task was already done. It had ushered in the Age of Steam.

The new engine was a success from the start. True, sometimes things went wrong: valves broke, steam leaked from inefficient casings, or the engineers got drunk and created chaos. But, all the same, orders for a Boulton & Watt engine came flowing in from all over the country. A distillery in London wanted one. So did a mine near Coventry, and another one in Scotland. And enquiries were already coming in from other countries.

The Cornish mine-owners wanted a fuel-saving Watt engine more than anyone else. It was, after all, not coal that they mined, but copper and tin. Instead of running their pumps on the very material they dug up, they had to bring every lump of their precious fuel in from outside the county. The cost was ruinous, but there was nothing they could do about it – until the Watt engine came on the scene.

At first, they tried to steal the design. Not long after the Bloomfield engine started work, a group of Cornishmen came to see it. When they left, one of them took with him a drawing that showed how everything worked.

Watt soon discovered the loss; Boulton, livid, wasted no time in taxing his visitors with what they'd done. Shamefacedly, they told him the drawing had been picked up by mistake. The man who'd taken it was a mine manager called Richard Trevithick: a name that Watt was to hear again!

Enough to last a lifetime

In the end, the Cornish had to settle for buying the machine, and they started by ordering two. Watt took charge of the installation, and soon found he'd heard enough of Trevithick, Cornish mines and Cornwall itself to last him a lifetime.

James Watt in 1792, at the age of fifty-six. By this time, his major work was behind him and he was part-owner of a prosperous business. A few years later, in 1800, he retired from the business but, to the end of his life in 1819, he continued to take an interest in the new world his own inventions had created.

Just getting there was horrendous enough. The inventor, who'd recently married again, set off with his new wife Ann in the summer of 1777. The two hundred-mile journey took them four days. Nor did the Watts find the Cornish at all welcoming.

On the contrary, they were rude, boorish, ignorant: "The enginemen actually eat the grease for the engine!" Watt wrote back despairingly to his Birmingham circle. Worse, many were deeply suspicious of this outsider and his newfangled contraption.

Watt worked on, trying both to ease the Cornish miners' doubts and to bring the two engines to working order. Of the two, he found the second task far, far easier. He'd never been good at socializing with strangers; he also loathed the business of making contacts, chatting people up, and generally creating interest in himself and his machine. But he had to do it; it was all part and parcel of being in business. And, in Cornwall, it was weary work.

Trevithick was actively insolent; the other managers were hostile, stupid or both. So it was an anxious moment when, a month after Watt's arrival, one machine was ready to run. Joy! It behaved itself, and went on behaving. The other went into operation a few months later. Little by little, the suspicions of the Cornish began to fade – and the orders to come in.

"The earth, which had been burrowed out by those human rabbits in their search after tin, lay around in huge ungainly heaps ... dirt and slush, and pools of water confined by muddy dams, abounded on every side; muddy men, with muddy carts and muddy horses, slowly crawled hither and thither."

Conditions above ground at Cornish tin mines, around the time that Watt knew them.

Wanted: new markets

James Watt had now shown the world how to harness steam power efficiently. And, as far as he was concerned, that was enough. He had his hands full, running the Cornish end of the business and making sure that his pump met the demands made on it. But the canny Boulton, far-sighted as ever, thought differently. He knew that Cornwall was only one market among many. Sooner or later, most of the Cornish mines would have Watt pumps – and what would happen to sales then?

The partnership had to expand, open up new markets, develop machines that were more powerful and efficient still. And Boulton also knew where these might be used. By this time, other "manu-factories" and works were springing up to join his own. Some, like Wilkinson's, made heavy ironware. Others, like Josiah Wedgwood's famous business, produced pottery. Others again produced textiles, especially cotton textiles.

Cotton, mills, and rotary motion

The cotton industry was then a very new one. Like mining, it was flourishing, and for a similar reason. New machines – new inventions like Richard Arkwright's mechanized spinning frame – were improving the productivity of textile manufacture beyond all recognition. True, the spinning machines in Arkwright's chain of textile mills were powered in the old way, by water. But, surely, that couldn't last for ever!

Something of all this was already in Boulton's mind as he watched the Bloomfield pump go into action. By that time, so the local newspaper man reported, he was planning to provide engines to meet "almost all Purposes where Mechanical Power is required, whether great or small, or where the Motion wanted is either rotatory or reciprocating."

"Rotatory" or reciprocating: obviously, that was the next step. Watt's pump, like Newcomen's before it, was a reciprocating engine. Its movement was two-way only: in and out, up and down, side to side. But so many machines – starting with the flour-mill and all its relatives – operated on the rotary principle. They went round and round. Could a Watt engine be built that worked like this?

"Steam mill mad"

In June 1781, Boulton wrote a tactful letter to his partner that has since become famous. "The people in London, Manchester and Birmingham," he told Watt, "are *steam mill mad.* I don't mean to hurry you but I think in the course of a month or two, we should determine to take out a patent for certain methods of producing rotative motion....

"There is no other Cornwall to be found, and

Steam and iron were the foundations of the Industrial Revolution of the late eighteenth century. Iron-making had a revolution of its own in 1709 when, at Coalbrookdale in England, Abraham Darby first made iron using coke as a furnace fuel. Previously, the furnaces had been fuelled with charcoal which, as forests were felled, had become scarce. The vast increase in iron production needed to make steam engines and, later, railways, would not have been possible without Darby's breakthrough.

the most likely line for the consumption of our engines is the application of them to mills which is certainly an extensive field."

With Watt, tact succeeded where nagging failed; something that Roebuck, who nagged badly, had never understood. Watt, aged forty-five, rose to the new challenge and, within a matter of months, produced a solution.

By October, he'd come up with a brand-new device that converted the movement into a rotary one. It had to be a new device, because someone else had already taken out a patent on the most obvious way of doing the job, by using a crank.

A crank is a wheel attached to a hinged rod: a to-and-fro movement of the rod will make the wheel go round, and vice versa. Barred from using this simple idea, Watt worked out something equally simple. He attached the "pump-handle", the overhead beam, to a long rod that ended in a small notched wheel. The beam's up-and-down movement made this wheel move round another one, which in its turn rotated a much larger wheel.

Thanks to this "sun-and-planet" gear, in which one wheel rotated round another, the original Boulton & Watt steam engine could be quickly transformed into the much more versatile rotative model. But Watt did not stop there. The new-style steam engine that he patented in 1782 differed in two major ways, not one, from the machine that had conquered Cornwall. Not only did it work by rotary motion; it worked twice as efficiently!

Pull-push action

Both Newcomen's pump and Watt's first engine had been "single-acting": that is, the power that drove them only functioned in one direction. It pulled the "pump-handle" down, at its end nearest the cylinder. It did not, however, push it up. Gravity did that, acting on the other end of the beam when the pull on the engine end was abandoned.

But the latest machine to be developed produced twice as much power for the amount of steam involved. By re-arranging its valve system, Watt had produced an engine that exerted power in two directions. This "double-acting" engine pulled the beam down *and* pushed it up again.

This pull-push action made another change necessary. Until then, the piston-rod and the beam had been joined by flexible chain linking. But this would not do now, since the chain could not transmit the upward thrust of the "push" movement. Watt now faced the problem of linking something that moved up and down – the piston rod – with something that moved through an arc of a circle: the end of the rocking-beam.

The straight line and the curve

It sounds trivial; in fact, it is fiendishly difficult. Confined to its up-and-down path, the rod cannot move sideways by the least amount. The beam-end, however, travels in a sideways curve. Somehow, Watt had to bring the rod's straight line and the beam's curve together. And he had to keep them together through all the different positions the

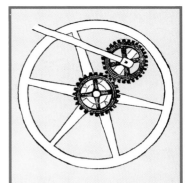

The "sun and planet" gear, a step on the road to a more efficient steam engine, transferring energy from one plane to another. It derived its name from the fact that the outer wheel rotated round the inner one like a planet round the sun.

"The wheel A is fixed at the end of an axis which carried a fly[wheel]; the wheel B is fixed fast to the connecting-rod from the working-beam, and cannot turn on its axis; and is confined by some means, so as always to keep in contact with the wheel A; consequently by the action of the engine it goes round it and causes it to revolve on its axis."

James Watt, describing the action of the "sun-and-planet" gear.

engine made them take up.

He first tried doing it by inter-connecting notches, like the ones on the gears. But the teeth of the notch system kept breaking – and breaking again. Something else was needed and, in the summer of 1784, he started playing with the geometry of the problem.

The beam-end traced an arc of one circle. Now, supposing a similar arc was traced of another circle, back-to-back with the first one, and directly under it? The two arcs would not, of course, make a straight line. But they were not far off.

Watt quickly translated this into mechanical terms. The second circle could be traced by the end of another beam, or rod, or anything straight. Then the moving ends of the two rods could be linked by a third. If the first rod – the beam – were moved through its usual arc, the second one would move as well. The short third rod, at its ends, echoed the arcs of the other two. But there was a point along its length which did not. That point, unlike anything else in the whole arrangement, *moved almost in a straight line.*

"A probable thing to succeed"

Watt wrote to Boulton on June 30, giving tentative news of success. "I have started a new hare!" he joked. "I have got a glimpse of a method of causing a piston-rod to move up and down perpendicularly, by only fixing it to a piece of iron upon the beam.... I have only tried it in a slight model yet, so cannot build upon it, though I think it a very probable thing to succeed."

And succeed it did. That single point on the third connecting rod was the place where the straight line and the circle met. When attached to it, the piston transmitted all its up-and-down thrust to the end of the beam. And the beam, moving along its arc, swung into the air.

In its final form, the equipment was more complicated but much more compact. When, aged seventy-two, Watt recalled the movement of its polished parallel rods, he could still glow with pride.

"I am not over anxious after fame," he told his son, also named James. "Yet I am more proud of the parallel motion than of any other mechanical invention I have ever made."

Towering achievements

The sun-and-planet gears, the double-acting engine, the parallel motion device: any single one of these would have been enough to cover its inventor with distinction. Taken together – and added to the initial invention of the separate condenser itself – they added up to a towering achievement. But, amazingly, they are only part of what James Watt created after he joined fortunes with Boulton.

Boulton went far beyond giving his partner financial security; he also gave him friendship, encouragement and an endlessly patient ear. (Watt, when feeling down, could be a great complainer!) Under his genial influence, the inventor's creativity flourished as never before.

There was, for instance, his patent copying process, which he developed at the end of the 1770s. This was a hundred years before the typewriter took a lot of the drudgery out of business correspondence, and very many more before the photocopier removed much of the rest. The only way that Boulton and Watt could take copies of the letters they wrote was to copy them out themselves – by hand. It was a time-wasting, tedious chore.

Watt decided that it had to stop and, very quickly, produced a whole letter-copying system, complete with special inks, special paper and special presses. It worked rather like a child's transfer does today. After writing a letter, the writer would carefully press a sheet of thin, absorbent paper down on top of the still-wet ink. When this upper sheet was peeled off, it carried a "transfer" of the letter, written in back-to-front, mirror-image script.

All the reader then had to do was turn the paper round. Because it was so thin, the writing showed through from the back ... the right way round.

Watt wasn't the only busy person to rebel against the need for hand-copying. Naturally, Boulton

"I have fallen on a way of copying writing chemically.... I can copy a whole-sheet letter in five minutes."

James Watt, on his copying process.

Above: Steam power applied to weaving resulted in the mass production of cheap textiles, though at the cost of poor conditions for the people – mainly women and children – who worked in the weaving mills.
Right: James Nasmyth's steam hammer, invented in 1839, revolutionized the forging of iron and made it possible to forge large machine parts accurately.

manufactured and promoted his partner's latest inspiration, and sold over a hundred in the first year alone. The Watt copier soon became part of standard business practice, and stayed in use for a hundred years.

How powerful is a horse?

Another spin-off from Watt's main work has been in use for much longer still. In 1782, a customer ordered an engine to drive a sawmill. Like any other miller at that time, he explained what he wanted in terms of horsepower: the amount of work that could be done by a horse, walking round and round a treadmill. The engine was to have the power of about twelve horses.

While this figure meant something to the mill-owner, it was hardly exact enough for Watt. Here was something that had to be worked out properly! How much power, for instance, did a horse really exert? How much work did a horse actually do?

Watt armed himself with the sawmill's figures: the distance a horse walked in a minute, the weight lifted by the machine it drove, and so on. Then he started calculating, and finally worked out that a horse could lift thirty-three thousand pounds the distance of one foot in one minute.

The inventor could now estimate how powerful the engine needed to be. More, he could now describe how powerful *any* of his machines were – and price them accordingly. He had defined a standard unit by which power could be measured: a unit that still has a place in the British imperial system of measurement. The international measurement system, however, uses a different unit for measuring power. It is called ... the watt.

A revolution in industry

So James Watt continued through his middle age, designing, improving, inventing, and improving on his own inventions. Meanwhile, the fame of his greatest invention of all was increasing by the year. Boulton's great gamble was paying off brilliantly,

"It has armed the feeble hand ... with a power to which no limits can be assigned; completed the dominion of mind over the most refractory qualities of matter; and laid a sure foundation for all those future miracles of mechanic power which are to aid and reward the labours of after generations."

James Watt's steam engine, described in his obituary, 1819.

"The great, unwearying power of the Watt engine made possible the mechanization of production methods upon a scale that was inconceivable before."

L.T.C. Rolt, from his biography, "James Watt".

Steam made Britain the world's leading industrial power until about 1880, when the United States caught up and eventually took the lead, with Germany close behind. In 1851 – when Britain's industrial strength was at its height – a Great Exhibition was held in Hyde Park in London. Its purpose was to show that Britain was "the workshop of the world". This illustration from the exhibition brochure shows a range of machinery that British industry and ingenuity had created.

for machines and the factories that housed them were completely revolutionizing industries. The revolution's leader was still cotton: light, comfortable, washable cotton. With machines like Arkwright's speeding production up, the price was falling all the time – and demand growing.

Among the factories' owners, demand was growing too: for something more powerful and much less chancy than a water-wheel to turn those busy spindles and bobbins. The Boulton & Watt rotative engine was all they wanted – and more. If a factory was equipped with a power source like this, it could be sited wherever the owner wished. Producers, if they paid Boulton & Watt's terms, could free themselves for ever from their old reliance on water, weather and the freaks of the landscape.

For the first time in history, workers could truly dominate their natural environment.

Left: The steam engine played an important part in the development of the iron industry. Steam was used to drive air through the furnaces and to drive forge hammers. It was largely thanks to steam that the output of the British iron industry – then the world's leader – almost quadrupled between 1788 and 1804.

By 1800, when Watt's main patent finally ran out, eighty-four British cotton mills were using Boulton & Watt engines. So were some wool mills, suddenly aware of the looming threat posed by their new rivals. And the flour-milling industry had begun to copy their example.

The Albion Flour Mills that Boulton set up in London had caused a sensation when they were put to work in the 1780s. They burned down in 1791, but not before the flour millers of Britain had got the hint. Like it or loathe it – and many of them loathed it – the steam engine and the huge amounts of power it made available were the keys to industry's future.

Planning to enjoy himself

The expiry of the patent also marked the formal end of the Boulton & Watt partnership. The two friends were now getting old – Boulton was seventy-two, Watt sixty-four – and their sons had taken over Soho's engine-making operations. Even so, Boulton did not even think of retiring: forward-looking to the end, he plunged into a new scheme for building machinery for minting coins. But James Watt had different plans.

Everything that, once, seemed so far out of reach had now been granted to him: wealth, fame, the recognition of his profession and his country ... and even good health. Happiness and good fortune, coming late but coming in the end, had banished the migraines that once made life a misery. He was now fit to enjoy retirement, and he took it.

Happy in a new house he'd built for himself, he spent the last nineteen years of his life doing all the things he liked best. He read; he researched; he planned a garden and planted it; and he spent hours in the workshop he'd rigged up for himself in the attic.

Here, surrounded by the tools he treasured all his life, he worked on his latest scheme – a machine for copying pieces of sculpture. This newest "hare" claimed all his attention, just as the rest had done. It absorbed him so much that, often, he didn't even

TREVITHICKS, PORTABLE STEAM ENGINE.

Catch me who can.

Mechanical Power Subduing Animal Speed.

come downstairs for meals. It would have meant tidying himself up ... and he couldn't really be bothered. Instead, standing over the attic stove, he would cook himself a snack.

Even before the century ended, his friends had started dying. Black was the first to go; then Robison, and then, in 1809, Boulton himself. Richard Trevithick, Watt's old adversary in Cornwall, died too. But Trevithick's role as an irritant to the firm of Boulton & Watt soon passed to his son, also named Richard and – like Watt himself – an engineer.

Even before the Watt patent expired, this younger Richard Trevithick began building steam engines with Watt-style separate condensers that harnessed a property of steam that Watt had not exploited: its expansive power. Soon, he was designing rotative steam engines that also worked on this high-pressure principle. His high-pressure engines worked well, so he then designed several others.

One of these was a full-sized, self-propelled steam-carriage which, in 1804, trundled along nine and a half miles of railed tracks in South Wales, pulling a train loaded with seventy passengers and ten tons of iron. It was the world's first railway locomotive.

Here was a rival who could put the Soho operation out of business for good! But the dangers of high pressure steam discouraged possible buyers (one of the steam engines exploded, killing four men), and Trevithick later left England to seek his fortunes in Peru. Meanwhile, Watt – if he knew about this threat to his life's work – had his mind on other things: on his greenhouses, and his tree-planting, and the tools in his attic.

James Watt died aged eighty-three, on August 25, 1819, and was buried close to his old partner, Matthew Boulton.

A legacy to the world

By increasing the power of humans, James Watt led society into some of the greatest changes it has ever seen. The Industrial Revolution – the shift from home-based craft work to factory-based mass

Opposite: Richard Trevithick – the son of Watt's old Cornish adversary – was the pioneer of the next stage of the steam revolution – the steam locomotive. His first successful locomotive ran in 1804 at an iron works in South Wales. In 1808, Trevithick gave a public demonstration of his latest locomotive, "Catch me who can", in London. But financial trouble overtook him, and it was left to George Stephenson and his son Robert to develop the steam locomotive to its full potential.

"The darkest side of this rapid power revolution was that it robbed the craftsman's hands of their cunning and subjected him to the swift, inhuman rhythm of the new machines."

L.T.C. Rolt, from his biography, "James Watt".

Steam changed the pace of transport during the nineteenth century. The first steamships were driven by paddle-wheels operated by a steam engine. On the Mississippi River in the United States, sternwheelers like the "Delta Queen" (above) carried goods and passengers. Steam railways had an impact on the countryside as they involved the building of bridges, tunnels and viaducts like the Stockport Viaduct (right) near Manchester, England.

production – was only one of them. Another was a revolution in travel and communications. A third was the huge population shift that took place as the new factories were set up and people moved in from the countryside to work in them.

The engines Watt built and the power he harnessed set these changes in motion well before he died. Later, as the process of change spread outwards in ever-widening circles, his legacy transformed people's lives out of all recognition. He shaped the nineteenth century as surely as if he'd lived through it. Remote but real, his influence still reaches out and touches us today.

The speed of change

Many of these changes came very fast. One of the biggest changes the increase of power brought about was that the pace of all change speeded up. As the results multiplied, it speeded up still further. But, to the bewildered onlookers of the early nineteenth century, even the earliest changes of all seemed to come almost overnight.

For instance, Trevithick's seventy passengers took their historic journey in 1804. Only four years later, his "Catch me who can" locomotive, which advertized itself as "Mechanical Power Subduing

In the United States steam engines had a distinctive appearance, with "cowcatcher" grids mounted in front of the wheels and tall, wide funnels. Both features reflected the environment in which the locomotives worked. The railways ran on unfenced track across vast areas of cattle country – hence the grids. They also passed through extensive forests, and the funnels were designed to prevent sparks escaping and setting fire to the trees.

Animal Speed", was carrying Londoners on joyrides around a circular track.

In 1814, an engineer, George Stephenson, produced a steam locomotive that hauled an eight-wagon train of coal *uphill*. In 1825, his more famous *Locomotion* carried a group of passengers along the world's first-ever public rail line. Five years later still, the even more celebrated *Rocket* made its prize-winning run on the Manchester and Liverpool Railway which – built by Stephenson himself – gave the world its first regular passenger rail service.

The Manchester and Liverpool was soon joined by others. By 1850 – less than half a century from that first ponderous trip achieved by Trevithick's engine – rail lines spidered out all across Britain.

No longer did the public face journeys like the ones endured by James Watt a hundred years earlier. Early train travel was still far from comfortable, but journey times could now be counted in hours rather than days.

Race of the steamships

It was the same fast-moving story with water transport – and, as with Watt's own steam-engine, the story started in Scotland. Steam was first used to power a ship in 1801, when the idea of the steam-powered paddle-wheel was applied to a canal boat, the *Charlotte Dundas*. The example set by this first paddle-steamer was quickly copied, especially in the United States, and, in 1819, the paddle-steamer *Savannah* made history for all time by becoming the first steamship to cross the Atlantic Ocean.

Two centuries earlier, this journey had taken two months or more. By 1838, when the paddle-steamers *Sirius* and *Great Western* challenged each other to an epic race, the time had been cut to well under three weeks. A hundred years later, it had dropped to three days.

Thanks to steam power, distance and time had lost their old links with wind, terrain and hurrying horses' hooves. To the dizzied onlookers, it must have seemed that the world was shrinking as they watched.

The making of industry

The changes this brought about were indeed dizzying. They included an extraordinary speed-up in communications, a massive increase in trade, an explosion in numbers emigrating to the New World, and some enormous changes in the attitudes of the people left in the old one. No longer was London – or Paris, or Berlin – like something out of a fable, a place from which few visitors returned. Provincial dwellers could now go and work there, settle there, marry someone there ... and still return regularly to see their families back home.

But, immense though these changes were, they were dwarfed by those that arose from steam power's impact on industry. In fact, steam power *made* industry, in the way we now understand the word. All industry used to be run from people's sheds, kitchens, and workshops.

Soon, large-scale manufacturing industries would begin to emerge and take the place of craftspeople. In Germany, the change took place in the 1850s and 1860s when there was a period of rapid growth. The railways expanded and basic industries, like mining, metals, textiles and iron, became large-scale concerns. Pig iron production rose from 529,000 tons in 1850 to two million tons in 1875.

"Workshop of the world"

Nor did the power revolution confine itself to mining, iron-making and textile manufacture. Steel, smelted from iron, was beaten, rolled or shaped on steam-powered machines. In the fields, steam-threshing machines quickly completed a task that, by hand, could take from harvest time till Christmas. Newspapers were printed on steam-driven presses. After the mid-century invention of the sewing-machine, parts of the clothing industry changed over to sewing clothes by steam.

Britain, home of the technology that made all this possible, earned itself the nickname "Workshop of the World". By the end of the nineteenth century, industrial world leadership had passed to Germany, then to the United States. But, by this time, Britain

"In most of our great manufactories these engines now supply the place of water, wind, and horse mills; and, instead of carrying the work to the power, the prime agent is placed wherever it is most convenient to the manufacturer."

James Watt, describing the double-acting rotative engine's impact on industry.

had changed roles to become the world's most powerful political leader: the ruler, as the Victorians boasted, of an "empire where the sun never sets".

Other Western nations acquired empires of their own and this land-grabbing was also linked to the revolution steam had brought about. They all needed the raw materials to feed their industries' machines; they also needed places where they could sell their industrial products. An empire of subject peoples, powerless to shake off their Western overlords, met both these needs.

Cities

Steam power changed the map of the world; it also changed the map of every country where it held sway. The towns where the factories were set up grew ... and grew ... and grew.

In 1750, for instance, the town where Matthew Boulton was working in his family firm consisted of about thirty thousand people. By 1801, the year after his partnership with Watt ended, the town's

Opposite and above: Steam paved the way for the next industrial revolution – the development of electric power. Electricity is generated by using steam pressure raised by coal, oil, natural gas or nuclear fuel to drive a turbine which, in turn, drives a generator. So the technology of even today's most modern power stations looks back to the principles worked out by Watt over two hundred years ago.

population had doubled. By the mid-century, it had shot up to well over two hundred thousand. The same story could be told throughout the industrialized world. In Germany, the population of Berlin increased by one hundred thousand between 1840 and 1850.

Slowly, Europeans and their descendants elsewhere were giving up their centuries-old links with the land. Instead, they were building societies based on quite a different way of life: on living in close quarters, collected together in a town.

The past and the future

Once people are collected together in large numbers, many things become possible that cannot happen easily in a sparsely-populated area. For instance, people can join together to demand better conditions. They can form powerful protest groups, political parties, even revolutionary armies.

Again, they can be helped more efficiently. It is easier for people to take advantage of health and education services in a big town than it is in remote countryside, where distances are big and travel is expensive and time-consuming. And, for just the same reasons, they can be sold things more efficiently. Businesses find it worth their while to suit their trade to a large urban population, since – if they get their calculations right – big sales can result.

In 1882, a business entrepreneur and inventor, Thomas A. Edison, found it worth his while to sell New York a system for bringing electrical power into the home...

With Edison, we bridge the technology gap between Watt's time and our own. Electricity brought the world out of the Age of Steam, and prepared the way for the high technology of the late 1900s. But Edison's system itself depended on steam for generating electricity. And the same is true of some power stations today.

James Watt, the engineer who shaped our past, will continue to shape our future far into the twenty-first century.

"The trunk of an elephant, that can pick up a pin or rend an oak, is as nothing to it. It can engrave a seal, and crush masses of obdurate metal before it, draw out, without breaking, a thread as fine as gossamer, and lift a ship of war like a bauble in the air. It can embroider muslin and forge anchors, – cut steel into ribbons and impel loaded vessels against the fury of the winds and waves."

The power of James Watt's steam engine, described in his obituary, 1819.

Important Dates

1698	Thomas Savery patents his "Miner's Friend": a water pump powered by creating and then condensing steam so as to form a vacuum.
1712	Thomas Newcomen sets up his first "atmospheric engine" – a fully-functioning steam pump.
1736	Jan 19: James Watt is born in Greenock, Scotland.
1755	Watt leaves Scotland to seek training as an instrument-maker in London. He is taken on by John Morgan of Cornhill.
1756	His training completed, Watt returns to Scotland and repairs an instrument collection for Glasgow University.
1757	Glasgow University sets Watt up as its official "Mathematical Instrument Maker", with a shop in the university grounds.
1763-4	Professor John Anderson brings Watt a model of a Newcomen pump for repair. Watt realizes that the pump works inefficiently because its cylinder has to be cooled and re-heated with every stroke.
1765	May: Watt, aged twenty-nine, works out the solution to the pump problem: a separate cooling chamber, or condenser. Later that year, he is introduced to scientist and industrialist John Roebuck, who is interested in developing Watt's invention for commercial use.
1769	Watt patents his "New Method of Lessening the Consumption of Steam and Fuel in Fire Engines". In the same year, Richard Arkwright patents his water-powered spinning machine, the "Water Frame".
1774	Watt, aged thirty-eight, moves from Scotland to Birmingham, England, and starts work at the Soho Manufactory as the partner of Matthew Boulton, bringing the steam engine he has designed into production.
1776	The Boulton & Watt steam pump makes its first working appearance in public, at the Bloomfield Colliery.
1777	Watt travels to Cornwall to set up Boulton & Watt pumps at two mines.
1781	Watt patents the vital component of his rotative engine, the sun-and-planet gear.
1782	Watt patents his double-acting engine. In the same year, he devises a standard unit of measurement for power: the horsepower.
1784	Watt's parallel motion device is patented.
1785	Edmund Cartwright, a clergyman, patents his powered weaving-loom. Together with powered spinning machines, already introduced, improved versions of the power-loom will play a leading role in taking manufacturing industries out of the home and into factories.
1800	Watt's patent on his steam engine runs out. The Boulton & Watt partnership comes to an end, and sixty-four-year--old Watt retires.
1804	The world's first steam-powered railway locomotive, designed by Richard Trevithick, hauls a load of ten tons of iron and around seventy people over a distance of more than nine miles.
1819	Aug 25: James Watt dies, aged eighty-three.

Scientific Terms

Arc: A section of a circle's circumference.

"Atmospheric engine": A machine powered by the *pressure* of the earth's atmosphere (the air), acting on a *vacuum* produced by condensing *steam:* the name given to Newcomen's pumping engine. Although Watt's engine used *steam* rather than air, it worked in the same basic way. See *condenser.*

Boiler: The part of a *steam* engine where water is converted into *steam.* The water in the boiler is heated until it boils.

Condense, condenser: When *steam* is cooled, it condenses, or turns back to water. Watt's greatest achievement was the invention of a separate cooling-chamber, or condenser, for the Newcomen pump.

Double-acting engine: See *single-acting engine.*

Energy: The capacity to do work.

Horsepower: Unit of measurement for power used in the British (imperial) measurement system. One horsepower equals 745.7 watts (see *Watt).*

Industrial Revolution: The massive changeover from home-based systems of production to factory-based ones that was pioneered in Britain in the late eighteenth and early nineteenth centuries. The key to the change was the introduction of powered machines (using water or *steam* power) to do work previously done by hand, such as spinning and weaving.

"Manufactory": A place where goods are made; the original version of the word "factory".

Patent: Legal protection, lasting for a fixed length of time, for an invention. While the patent lasts, only the patent-holder has the right to make goods using the invention, and to market them.

Piston, piston-rod: A piston is a circular piece of metal, cut to fit closely inside a cylinder and free to move up and down. The piston-rod is a rod attached at right-angles to the piston.

Pivot: A short rod on which something turns.

Power: In scientific language, the rate at which work is done, or *energy* is used up or produced. In ordinary speech, "power" is often given the meaning that actually belongs to *"energy":* the ability to do work. A machine that is "powered" by *steam* is in fact a machine that uses the *energy* of *steam* to do the job it was designed for.

Pressure: Force exerted against something. The piston of the Newcomen pump was driven down in to the pump's cylinder by the pressure of the atmosphere exerted against its upper surface.

Quadrant: An instrument for measuring angles.

Reciprocating: Two-way, straight-line motion: up and down, or side to side. Compare with *rotary.*

Rotary, rotative: Circular motion; an engine operating in this way.

Single-acting/double-acting engines: In a single-acting engine, *pressure* is exerted on the *piston* on one side only: the upper one, in the case of the Newcomen and early Watt pumps. In double-acting engines, like the later Boulton & Watt ones, the *pressure* is exerted, first on one side of the *piston,* then on the other.

Steam: The gas into which water turns when it is boiled. When this happens, its volume expands 1700 times. When steam in a container is *condensed,* it contracts again, creating a *vacuum* in the space it once filled. Both Newcomen and Watt based their engine designs on this *vacuum*-creating property of steam. Later on, however, engineers changed over to exploiting steam's expansive *power.* Early examples of this use of high-*pressure* steam include the first railway locomotives.

Sun-and-planet gear: A gear system involving two wheels, one of which drives the other by moving around it.

Turbine: A slatted wheel or circular device turned by the movement of a fluid or gas over the slats. A *steam* turbine is driven by *steam.*

Vacuum: Space which has been totally or to a large extent emptied of matter.

Valve: A device which can be opened and closed (either by hand or automatically) to control the movement of fluid or gas through a narrow passage.

Watt: The International System (SI) unit of *power,* named after James Watt. One watt is equal to one joule per second. (The joule is the SI unit of *energy.*)

"The great, unwearying power of the Watt engine made possible the mechanization of production methods upon a scale that was inconceivable before."

L.T.C. Rolt, from his biography, "James Watt".

"It has armed the feeble hand ... with a power to which no limits can be assigned; completed the dominion of mind over the most refractory qualities of matter; and laid a sure foundation for all those future miracles of mechanic power which are to aid and reward the labours of after generations."

James Watt's steam engine, described in his obituary, 1819.

"Watt could not foresee the historical consequences of his work and did not attempt to do so. Hence the tragic paradox of the industrial revolution, that while wealth accumulated, people decayed."

L.T.C. Rolt, from his biography, "James Watt".

"Machinery permits the introduction of a great number of children of both sexes.... The hours of work are made to surpass all bounds; and, for the daily bait of a few pence, minds, which education would enlighten, are sacrificed to enduring brutalization, whilst the bodily frame is blighted for want of that development which the enjoyment of the air and sun rarely fails to bring along with it."

A French opponent of children working in factories, 1839.